7.09 X

MANAGING
AND RESOURCES

& HIGHE

Also available:

Baby and Toddler Development Made Real
Sandy Green (1-84312-033-X)

Essential Skills for Managers of Child-Centred Settings
Emma Isles-Buck and Shelly Newstead (1-84312-034-8)

Planning an Appropriate Curriculum for the Under Fives
Rosemary Rodger (1-85346-912-2)

Other titles in the same series:

Self-development for Early Years Managers
Chris Ashman and Sandy Green (1-84312-197-2)

Managing People and Teams
Chris Ashman and Sandy Green (1-84312-198-0)

Planning, Doing and Reviewing
Chris Ashman and Sandy Green (1-84312-199-9)

MANAGING ENVIRONMENT AND RESOURCES

Chris Ashman and Sandy Green

Illustrations by Dawn Vince

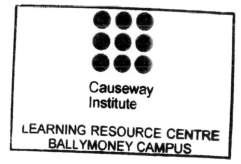

David Fulton Publishers

David Fulton Publishers Ltd
The Chiswick Centre, 414 Chiswick High Road, London W4 5TF

www.fultonpublishers.co.uk

First published in Great Britain in 2005 by David Fulton Publishers

10 9 8 7 6 5 4 3 2 1

Note: The right of the individual contributors to be identified as the authors of their work has been asserted by them in accordance with the Copyright, Designs and Patents Act 1988.

David Fulton Publishers is a division of Granada Learning, part of ITV plc.

British Library Cataloguing in Publication Data
A catalogue record for this book is available from the British Library.

ISBN 1 84312 200 6

Typeset by FiSH Books, London
Printed and bound in Great Britain

CONTENTS

ACKNOWLEDGEMENTS

Finance, resources and the environment weren't what attracted me to management – but during the past twenty years or so I have learnt the value of being good enough at understanding budgets and financial plans, of considering the environmental impact of decisions, and of the effect they have on the practical implementation of visions and ideas. Thanks for my education in these matters goes to many people in Croydon Social Services 1986–1993, Jo Barber at Norton Radstock College, the senior managers at Bridgwater College, and the best pair of role models during my childhood (in the self-employed business sense), my Mum and Dad.

The benefits and pitfalls of health and safety have also been a dramatic learning curve for me, and I have benefited from the shared experience and knowledge of many colleagues and trade-union officials. Special thanks goes to Pete Skinner for his ideas and for reviewing the manuscript.

Gina and our children Olivia and Jamie continued to give me the joy of family life and the much needed balance and energy to keep going.

Chris Ashman

Over the past 30 years it has been my privilege to work with practitioners and owners within many different early years settings, sharing in the joys and problems experienced in everyday early years practice. These links have without a doubt enriched my understanding of management, its requirements and its issues.

Being married to John, a huge influence and support in my life, and also working with Chris for several years has opened my eyes to some of the difficulties faced by managers in general, and the similarities between different management issues, not just those encountered within early years work.

Sandy Green

INTRODUCTION

This book is written for you if you are a manager, or are thinking of becoming one, within the Early Years sector. It provides an introduction to aspects of managing the working environment and resources. Much of the content could be applied to other sectors, as the role of manager can be generic. However, the examples and flavour of the ideas are set within a childcare context.

THE ENVIRONMENT AND RESOURCES

Your experience and training in Early Years will provide you with an understanding about the effect and impact of the environment on the development of children and their opportunity to thrive. A wide range of elements makes up this concept of the 'environment'. In a similar way, for a manager many things make up the working environment, some of which will be more important in your setting than others. Included within the definition of environment in this book are:

❏ The working space for children, staff and others
❏ Equipment that is used within the setting
❏ Working practices that may have an impact on children, other staff and visitors
❏ Services provided to children and staff, e.g. food and drink
❏ Other health and safety legislation matters

How comfortable are you using numbers, i.e. doing maths?

For some people this question may drain away a bit of the professional confidence they have built up during their vocational development. For others the answer will be more positive.

If you feel more in the former camp than the latter, be reassured you are not alone. It might not be that you are weak at using numbers within your work, but you may feel that you could improve.

Within this book there is a chance to explore how a manager can use numbers to help them manage more effectively. A few worked examples provide you with ideas to apply to your own level of responsibility – and give you some of the answers to check your own under-standing.[1]

There are some fundamental managerial responsibil-ities, such as keeping within the law. This is vital for the longer-term survival of your service provision and your career. Within the text you will have a chance to consider the benefits of going further than compliance with the law, of making your service stand out from the rest because it offers a well-resourced, carefully managed, health-promoting and safe setting where children and staff can thrive and reach their potential.

---

[1] The 'Skills for Life' initiative has some other great help and opportunities to support you in developing your skills and confidence in using numbers and communications. Contact your local college of further education or consult www.dfes.gov.uk/readwriteplus/learning

Chapter 1

MONEY MATTERS

This chapter covers:

- Useful methods to help you manage money
- How to set a budget and monitor spending
- Managing income and expenditure

Some people are spenders and others savers! Managers need to be good at both things: spending time, money and resources to get the job done as efficiently and effectively as possible; and saving energy, time and resources to reinvest in other activities.

Some people are very comfortable using numbers in their daily life and their working environment. Others may have an instant reaction of 'I can't do the maths!'

Who is the role model?

As an Early Years manager you will already work with numbers and money. As with other things, the more you use and practise the skills the more comfortable you will feel about using them.

USEFUL METHODS TO HELP YOU MANAGE MONEY

Planning is a skill you already possess. Within your practitioner role you will have developed methods to create ideas, organise activities and identify ways of evaluating outcomes for a whole range of curriculum-related actions. Managing money will call on many of these skills. When planning finance or money, management budgets will be used to set out aims and then monitor progress.

Definition

Budgets are plans that relate to activities measured by numbers.

Do not be afraid of your budget! It is a very useful system to control resources.
Examples of budgets will include:

❑ Ratios – lists of the total number of children in an age range compared to the total of qualified and unqual-ified staff on duty
❑ Salary costs – of employing staff
❑ Estimates – of the bills expected for consumables or gas, electricity, water, etc.

In this chapter it will be the budgets that we focus on. Understanding and using such financial plans and monitoring processes are vital aspects of any manager's successful career. It may not seem exciting to be a good financial manager, but even if your curriculum activities or your support of parents is superb, you still need to be solvent to carry on next year.

Setting a budget

Often you will be asked to set a budget, to create a plan, alongside other managers. Depending upon the size of the organisation that you work for, the budgets may be set by financial experts, the senior manager or owner of the service.

Even if you are not directly involved in deciding what goes into a budget plan it is important for you to have an understanding of how budgets are set. Such an understanding helps you to manage it more efficiently and effectively.

There are two broad approaches to setting a budget that can be categorised as (a) annual update and (b) blank sheet.

Annual-update budgets
When planning personal spending many people will go through a process similar to this, perhaps on a monthly basis:

- ❑ I need to know how much money I will receive – e.g. monthly salary
- ❑ Allocate regular expenses that are fixed – e.g. rent or mortgage, insurance
- ❑ Allocate money for other regular expenses that may

vary from month to month – e.g. food bills, entertainment, travel and transport, savings or paying off debts.

Some people do this as a conscious activity by getting bank statements, salary slips, utility bills, shopping receipts or other documents and working out the difference between income (salary) and expenditure (outgoings). Other people do something less consciously, but they have to do something to make sure that over time they have the money to spend on necessary things as well as desirable things.

Managers need to consciously plan and check the money. Taking the less conscious approach is inappropriate. Remember that as a manager the money you are dealing with, whether it is in the form of cash or resources, is other people's money. If you get it wrong, other people will care!

If you follow the approach of the budget updater you will look back at the last period (month or year) and plan in that light, making any sensible adjustments.

SCENARIO CASE STUDY

Budget time again had arrived at the 'Sure Footed Early Years Centre'. Karen was sitting down to prepare her staffing budget and her equipment budget for the next 12 months.

'Well,' Karen said to Denise, 'five staff, same as last year. We budgeted £67,500 for staff last year so with a planned pay rise of 2.5 per cent that will be £69,188 for next year. Then we spent £8,523 on equipment and materials, so with a bit for inflation that will go to £8,700.'

'That was quick,' said Denise. 'I don't know why people think that this budget planning stuff is so difficult.'

ACTIVITY 1.1

Think about the 'update budget' approach. Note down some of the good things that you consider this approach offers. Also try to identify any limitations that it may have in terms of effective and efficient management.

_____

_____

_____

_____

_____

Comment

You may have considered benefits such as:

❏ It's quick – by simply looking at last year's figures you can make a judgement for any change and set a budget
❏ It's based on actual events – because last year's spending actually occurred it provides some concrete experience to help you set a realistic budget for next year

You may also have identified limitations of this approach, including:

❏ Past events may not act as good predictors for the future – last year may have been particularly heavy or light in terms of spending. Did the budget that was set need adjusting during the year? Was it kept to, or significantly over- or under-spent? Will this year's budget need to put right something from last year's decisions?
❏ Efficiency and effectiveness of managers may be affected by this system – managers may be encouraged into a 'spend it or lose it' mindset.

ACTIVITY 1.2

Read this case study and consider what the appropriate managerial response to this scenario should be.

SCENARIO CASE STUDY

'Oh my word! Only six weeks until the end of the financial year,' cried Megan. 'I must ask the team for ideas to use up the rest of the budget.' She mentioned this to Bobbie. 'Why not save it?' asked Bobbie.

'Because we'll lose it! You know what those finance people are like. They won't even say "Well done", and what's more they'll reduce next year's budget as well because they think that we can manage on less!'

'Right. Get those catalogues out now!' enthused Bobbie.

_____

_____

_____

Comment

Megan and Bobbie have reacted as many managers working in this situation do. Working within a system like this, it appears that to be efficient as well as effective is penalised by having less in the future. It would be more appropriate to prioritise the needs of the service, consider whether the budget set at present levels is what the future period may require. Then armed with this information, to have a reasoned discussion with the finance manager. If savings can be made that should be greeted with a positive reaction. You may need to emphasise the future expectations you have (not to lose resources as a result). By doing this you have laid foundations of trust between you and the finance manager. Very soon you will be able to tell whether the finance manager is also trusting in you!

As a good manager you want to find ways to be more efficient. Wasting money, time or other valuable resources should be against our whole approach and ethos.

As a good manager you also need to be effective and get the job done well.

It is a balance that can best be considered in terms of saving and investing. If you save money by not spending it on something, is that positive for the organisation and its future, or is it a lack of investment in the future? An example that can illustrate the point is spending on training costs for staff or on maintenance of buildings and equipment. If you don't budget for training and development needs of staff, will that short-term saving be good for the service in the medium term, or will it have a negative impact upon practice, reputation or registration? If you cut back on mainte-nance of the building and fabric of the service ('Who notices if I spend money on clearing gutters and checking the roof?'), will that be more money to use directly on the children or will it cause even more expense in the future when repairs and replacements are required?

As usual within management the answer is uncertain. In different circumstances either decision may be correct or it may be questionable. The process of budget setting at least gives you the focus to consider what is the right thing to do.

Blank-sheet budgets

An alternative to the annual-update approach to setting budgets is the blank-sheet approach.

Rather than creating a plan based on the last period, managers using the blank-sheet approach will start by looking forward. To do this you will need to have a clear idea about what you expect in the future – e.g. the number of staff and the likely salary costs, the amount of electricity the service will consume, the number of children who will require lunches and how much providing these meals will cost.

The list will go on to cover all aspects of expenditure for your service. The advantage of this approach is that you need to think about what you are planning to do, not just think about what you did last year.

The previous year's budgets will certainly help. The headings that you have previously used can act as a prompt to make sure that you don't miss out anything that needs to have a budget for the next year. This is only the starting point, however. The blank-sheet approach means that you will have to delete headings that are no longer needed and add expenditure plans for new activities or costs.

Linking back to other plans, for example strategic and operating plans for the service, will be crucial to make sure everything planned is included.

It is also a useful safeguard to share your budget planning with others who may remind you of other things to include.

Useful budget headings

For experienced managers, setting budgets can be a routine activity. If you are new to the process the following activity should help you to explore the range of headings that your full budget may require.

ACTIVITY 1.3

Think about your service and the range of activities that the children and staff are involved in. Note down ideas for sub-headings that need money to be allocated under each of the suggested main headings.

Staff   **Equipment**

_____

_____

_____

_____

Now consider the environment that your service operates within. What other costs are there that need to be in the budget plan?

Building   **Running Costs**

_____

_____

_____

_____

Are there other things that need to be included?

_____

_____

Comment

Depending upon the specific service that you are dealing with, the list will be slightly different. Many managers will have identified sub-headings that include:

Staff

Salaries for each post
Ongoing costs for salaries
(e.g. national insurance,
pension contributions)
Sick-pay costs
Cover/replacement
Training and staff
development
Recruitment

Equipment

Capital items (e.g. fridge,
cooker, computer)
Consumable items (e.g.
paper, stationery, nappies,
cleaning items)

Building

Repairs and maintenance
Improvements

Running Costs

Energy bills
Cleaning

Others

Insurance

PLANNING A BUDGET – YOUR MATHS AND YOUR CREATIVITY

The process of setting your budget will require you to combine a number of skills and approaches as a manager. You will need to do the sums and check the maths. You will also need to apply your skills of foresight.

Here is a chance to have a go. The following scenario sets out a context for you to work through and ends up asking you to set a reasonable budget.

ACTIVITY 1.4

Background:
You are the manager of a team within an Early Years setting. You are asked by your line manager to 'take a look at the budgets for the year ahead'. You know that any savings on costs will be gratefully received. You also know that you will be expected to manage your team to deliver a consistently high-quality service to the children in your care.

Last year the starting budget looked like this:

HEADING	DETAIL	£	Subtotal £	Total £

STAFF

Team manager	1 post	17,500		
Practitioners (qualified)	2 posts	26,000		
Assistants (unqualified)	2 posts	19,000		
Salary on-costs		12,500		
Staff development		1,000		
Recruitment and cover		1,000		
				77,000

EQUIPMENT

Stationery		125		
Telephone		260		
Postage		80		
Books and software		120		
Craft materials		200		
Care resources		350		
Cleaning materials		95		
			1,230	
Capital items		500		
			500	
				1,730

RUNNING COSTS

Electricity		195		
Gas		85		
Water rates		133		
Refuse collection		95		
Cleaning service		2,200		
				2,708

BUILDING

Maintenance charge		1,500		
Repairs – minor and decoration		400		
				1,900

OTHER COSTS

Insurance		337		
Inspection preparation		100		
				437
				83,775

Using the budget information consider your approach to the following points. You know that you need to budget for:

❏ 2 per cent salary rise (don't forget that will change the 'on costs' of the salaries)
❏ Running costs will probably increase by 2.5 per cent next year
❏ Energy costs may rise by 4 per cent
❏ Insurance is set to rise by 12 per cent
❏ You are also aware that the curriculum developments will need new and replacement books and other learning resources
❏ Occupancy last year averaged at 65 per cent of capacity. After discussions with your manager you know that this needs to rise to closer to 85 per cent.
❏ One of your qualified practitioners has just left. You are covering the post by altering shift patterns and borrowing staff from other teams where occupancy allows.
❏ The recent inspection resulted in a plan that includes the need for more effective staff awareness of equality of opportunities and child-protection issues
❏ The main room your team work in is now looking shabby and tired. Staff have suggested a painting party or applying to a television make-over show.
❏ Parents have donated items of equipment for play, although some can't be used as they don't meet health and safety standards

Given these factors, how are you going to prepare your budget for the coming year? Use the blank table below to map out your ideas.

HEADING	DETAIL	£	Subtotal £	Total £

STAFF

Team manager				
Practitioners (qualified)				
Assistants (unqualified)				
Salary ongoing costs				
Staff development				
Recruitment and cover				

EQUIPMENT

Stationery				
Telephone				
Postage				
Books and software				
Craft materials				
Care resources				
Cleaning materials				
Capital items				

RUNNING COSTS

Electricity				
Gas				
Water rates				
Refuse collection				
Cleaning service				

BUILDING

Maintenance charge				
Repairs – minor and decoration				

OTHER COSTS

Insurance				
Inspection preparation				

Comment

Did you use an annual-update or blank-sheet approach? What factors from the Activity bullet points did you take into account and against which headings? You may have left a previous heading out (e.g. inspection) or increased another above the general percentage rise (e.g. books).

What other factors did you identify that you would need to find out about to set a realistic budget?

You may have considered income or what was actually spent rather than this starting-point budget.

If you have started to ask these and other questions you are ready to move on to thinking about how a plan can be monitored and used to help you manage effectively as well as efficiently.

MONITORING AND CONTROLLING EXPENDITURE

To have a plan is good. To use a plan to monitor what is really happening during a period of time is even better.

The best plans will need to be updated and modified as the realities of working life are encountered, surprises dealt with and opportunities grasped.

Once you have a budget agreed and in place the real job of tracking progress against that plan can start.

Your organisation should have its own system and process for doing this. It is vital to find out what this is and how your responsibilities are connected with it.

Below is a framework that could be used to help you monitor actual progress against your budget plan.

Every organisation incurs expenditure, spends money, places orders that commit spending, or consumes resources that will result in future bills.

Some spending will be equally spread through the year, e.g. salary payments. Others will be related to particular activities, e.g. purchases of equipment.

A monthly (sometimes weekly) summary of progress is often constructed to keep up to date with the position.

Some basic information is needed to do this:

❏ How much is in the budget?
❏ At this point in time how much would we expect to have spent?
❏ At this point in time how much have we spent (or made a commitment to spend)?
❏ What is the difference between what we planned and what we are actually committed to spend?

One way of setting this out is shown in the following table:

Name of Budget: Date: after 3 months
(e.g. Consumables & Equipment)

Details	Annual budget	Allocation to date	Actual to date	Variance	Variance %
Stationery	£125	£32	£39	–£7	–22
Telephone	£260	£65	£77	–£12	–18
Postage	£80	£20	£18	£2	10
Books and software	£120	£55	£69	–£14	–25
Craft materials	£200	£80	£113	–£33	–41
Care resources	£350	£88	£70	£18	20
Cleaning materials	£95	£23	£31	–£8	–35
Totals	£1,230	£363	£417	–£54	–15

In this table you can:

❏ See the plan in terms of the annual budget (column 2)
❏ See a detailed plan as set out by what was expected to be spent by the end of the third month (column 3)
❏ Monitor the actual activity by reading the actual to date (column 4)
❏ See how you are doing by comparing the actual position with the planned position (columns 5 in cash terms and 6 as a percentage)

ACTIVITY 1.5

Reading the budget is as important a management skill as writing a budget. Looking at the data in the table for 'Consumables and Equipment' what information can you find?

_____

_____

_____

_____

_____

Comment

You may have identified information such as:

❏ Overall the budget is overspent at this point in the year by £54, representing 15 per cent of the overall budget to date
❏ Only 'care resources' and 'postage' are underspent
❏ Craft materials and cleaning materials are the biggest overspends in percentage terms

❏ 'Craft materials' is the biggest overspend in cash terms, followed by books and telephone costs

In addition this information may prompt you to ask further questions. These are the questions about quality that, as a manager, you will want to explore because, as you know, efficiency (controlling costs) does not always equal effectiveness (getting the right things done well).

❏ Why are the care resources under-spent? It could be under-occupancy, or a shift of age-group numbers, or a change in demand from parents or practice from staff.

❏ Why are the cleaning, craft and book budgets overspent? It could be that the usual patterns of purchasing new equipment and resources at the beginning of the year are not reflected in the 'budget to date' profile.

❏ Why are both stationery and telephone budgets overspent? It could be that the controls for over-use are not tight enough or that the trends for use at certain points of the year are not reflected in the profile.

THE IMPORTANCE OF INCOME

Control of expenditure is a vital management skill to develop. Equally important is the other side of the economic seesaw, the income.

Everything that you can spend has to be covered and, in most cases, exceeded by income.

ACTIVITY 1.6

Think about the income streams that are possible for your service. How many things can you identlfy as actual or potential sources of income?

_____

_____

_____

Comment

Some of the usual income sources that you may have identified include:

❑ Fees from parents
❑ Government support in parental grants
❑ Project or government-initiative money
❑ Sponsorship from businesses
❑ Voluntary fundraising
❑ Donations
❑ Rent from hiring out facilities

Some of these sources may be more obvious than others, while some will be more significant in terms of amounts and regularity. However, they may all represent actual or potential sources of income.

In the same way as you prepare a budget for expenditure, you will need to plan a budget for expected income.

If, as for most Early Years services, your main sources are fees and government grants you will need to set realistic occupancy targets to allow you to identify target levels for income. The significance of occupancy rates and related income will be something that you will want and need to get very close to. Target setting and monitoring of income will inform you about the viability of the expenditure budgets that you have. If, during the year, it becomes obvious that income targets will not be met then expenditure plans will need to be reviewed. Alternatively you may identify that income targets will be exceeded and therefore the variable running costs of the service (things that reflect the number of children you provide a service for, such as food, drink and care supplies) will be higher than planned.

SCENARIO CASE STUDY

'Wow, we've been busy this week! What's the occupancy rate been, Jo?' asked a tired Mandy.

Jo looked at the statistics for the past month.

'Well, on average we've had 92 per cent of full occupancy. So that's up on the previous month where we had 85 per cent,' said Jo.

'Maybe we'll get a bonus then,' joked Mandy.

'Mmm,' pondered Jo. 'On the figures I've done we need to have an annual average of 87 per cent just to cover what it costs to run the place. So I wouldn't start spending that bonus quite yet!'

THERE'S MORE TO MONEY THAN CASH

As a developing manager it is good to be aware of financial matters other than income and expenditure. Your next stage of research could be to find out about capital projects and the financing of these larger-scale activities.

As a business it sometimes makes sense to borrow money to invest. This type of financing is often entered into when you perceive an opportunity to take advantage of, or a threat to avoid, in your service's local market. To borrow money to pay for the running costs of the existing business would be an indicator that things are going wrong. The income should always pay for the running costs, plus contribute to investment into future projects. To borrow to pay for running costs can soon become a longer-term disaster. If you need to borrow money to keep the service open week by week, then something is fundamentally wrong with your business plan.

The use of the PEST and SWOT analyses[1] can help you to identify future threats or opportunities that your service may encounter. Many businesses do not have enough current savings to invest in capital or equipment needed to survive any threats or take advantage of the opportunities. In these cases other organisations may be willing to lend money. This willingness will be based upon a risk analysis of lending the money and an expectation that interest will be paid on the loan. Therefore, the manager responsible within the service who is borrowing the money needs to be

---

[1] Political, Economic, Social, Technical and Strengths, Weaknesses, Opportunities, Threats. For more detail, see another of our books in the Managing in the Early Years series, *Planning, Doing and Reviewing.*

very confident that the investment is worthwhile for the business, can increase income to allow for the loan and interest to be repaid, and does not put undue strain on the rest of the business that may result in running out of money for the continuing provision of childcare.

Such decisions are very important to get right. You may not be involved in making such decisions yet, but being aware that other managers are may help you understand why, on occasions, your simple question may not get a quick answer.

IS YOUR NUMBER UP?

Why are so many people worried by numbers? If you are one of the many who find yourself avoiding the mathematics involved in managing money (personal or business), don't be too hard on yourself. It appears to be a national issue. You will of course be helping to combat this common weakness by the implementation of a curriculum designed to support number skills in children from Early Years onwards. While you should not be too hard on yourself, that does not mean that as a manager you should not identify your own learning needs and do something about improving your skills and performance.

As with other skills the more you practise, the easier it becomes. The quicker you find someone, or something, which can help you, starting at your level of knowledge and comfort, the more effective your learning will be. So be brave enough to seek support to develop any weakness you feel in your use and management of numbers. Your local further education college or adult and community learning services will be able to help.

REVIEW OF – MONEY MATTERS

This chapter has helped you if you can

- ✓ Set a budget using two different approaches.
- ✓ Use a monitoring system to spot where a budget is over- or under-spent.
- ✓ Explain the significance of income and expenditure as a manager.
- ✓ Demonstrate an awareness of when borrowing money is an investment as opposed to a mistake.

Chapter 2

MANAGING TO BE HEALTHY AND SAFE

This chapter covers:

- A broad introduction to the legislative framework
- Your main responsibilities as a manager
- The importance of assessing risks

If you want to find out about health and safety (and this you must do), one useful source would be to read the information provided by the Health & Safety Executive,[1] who are *the* authority on the subject within the UK. It is a frequently changing area of management that must never be compromised.

The purpose of this chapter is to provide you with some of the main themes you need to consider and set you thinking about managing so that your service is healthy and safe for the children, your staff and for others.

---

[1] HSE website: www.hse.gov.uk

LEARNING BY DOING

You already know that children, as well as adults, can learn very effectively from experience. This practical approach can, however, result in costly mistakes if left to its own devices. A child will certainly find out about the properties of heat by experience if left alone with fire, but no one would ever advocate such an unsupervised and uncontrolled risk.

For some people the successful management of health and safety is measured by the elimination of risk. However, children's knowledge and understanding will be limited if their experience is risk free. The same is usually true for adults. As with many matters in management there is a balance to be found between reasonable risk and effective learning. And it is only after the event that you can evaluate whether the balance was correct!

Using foresight rather than being convicted by hindsight

Being a good manager is usually a consequence of a combination of factors being present, in a mix that works, in any given situation. Consider the importance of the following factors:

❏ Professional or technical skills of the manager
❏ Relevant experience of the manager
❏ Luck – being in the right place at the right time
❏ Having good colleagues and team members
❏ Choosing the right option
❏ Interpersonal skills of the manager
❏ Intuition
❏ Having an opportunity to invest

You will have your own view about the relative importance of these, or other, factors that can contribute to someone being a good manager.

Whatever the magical mix is, you, as the manager, will need to develop and continually refine these various factors to achieve a balance that is appropriate to your setting. The test will be whether you get things right more times than you get them wrong, and whether you get the big decisions right!

A good manager needs only to make one BIG mistake for it all to go wrong. Within the area of safety and health there are many such BIG decisions to be made.

ACTIVITY 2.1

Use the space to develop the 'spider' gram. Identify some of the main responsibilities you have as a manager within the area of health and safety within an Early Years service. Add as many new lines or boxes as you can identify.

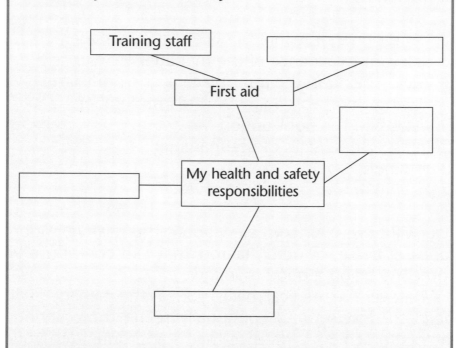

Comment

This may have been a difficult activity to get started on, but one that will continue to grow as your thinking and experience widens. Come back to it from time to time and add further ideas.

The following diagram may reflect some of your own ideas.

The following sections will provide an introduction to some of these themes. Once again you will need to research the latest legal and best-practice regulations that are applied to health and safety at work and within Early Years provision specifically.

MANAGEMENT OF HEALTH AND SAFETY

The legislative framework:

Health and Safety at Work etc. Act 1974 (1999)
European Union Regulations

Health and Safety at Work etc. Act 1974

This is the main piece of law that, along with European Union regulations, provides the framework for all health and safety good practice. It was a very important addition to the legal framework when it incorporated much of the previous specific items of law that covered industries like the railways or factory work into something that encompassed every workplace. From this date it didn't matter if you worked in heavy industry, in the science-based sector, with machines or children or animals, or in offices and factories. You were covered as the employer and the employee.[2]

The Health and Safety at Work etc. Act was also important as it set out the responsibilities of employers and their representatives (you as a manager take on this employer responsibility), as well as employees. The etc.

_____

[2] The only exception was work within the armed forces.

part is also an often left out but vital element. It represents the inclusion of everyone else who is not either an employer or employee. Visitors, sub-contractors, even intruders are covered by the law. The workplace must not present unreasonable risks to anyone who may be there.

Management health warning: the employer's responsibility

Within the law the manager or person with management responsibility takes on many of the employer's roles. It would not be any defence if things went wrong to say 'I'm only the team leader. I couldn't do anything about...' The question would be, as the team leader, what reasonable steps should you have taken.

This is why the responsibilities for ensuring health and safety are part of every job description. For all of us are covered as employees and you may also be involved as a representative of the employer as well.

So it is worth taking this very seriously – in order to avoid damage, illness or injury, of course, but also to avoid legal consequences.

Employees and their responsibilities
The Act sets out a clear framework for staff as employees of an organisation. By doing this, the legislation demonstrates that along with employers everyone has a significant role in making sure that the place of work is as healthy and as safe for everyone as it should be. No Early Years practitioner would dream of tolerating a situation that would harm a child, in the short or long term. The same principle must drive this area of management.

ACTIVITY 2.2

Consider the role of an employee. What would you expect to be the main responsibilities that employees have in relation to health and safety?

_____

_____

_____

_____

Comment and exploration

The law states that as an employee at work a person has a duty 'to take reasonable care for the health and safety of himself and of other persons who may be affected by his acts or omissions'.[3]

It is important to note that what you do (acts) and what you fail to do (omissions) are both included. So if you do something to cause an accident or if you don't do something that could have prevented an accident, the law judges that you are at fault. This sentence also covers yourself as well as other people as the subject of protection from the law. In addition this sentence also brings to our thinking the concept of 'reasonable'. The framework that is provided by the Health and Safety at Work etc. Act can be applied to so many different working environments because it sets out principles and general responsibilities. It leaves people to work out the specifics – for example, to define 'reasonable care' within a particular situation.

This section of the Act also requires employees to

---

[3] Health and Safety at Work etc. Act 1974, section 7, 'General duties of employees at work'.

do what they are instructed to do by their employer in regard to health and safety procedures. While at work you, as an employee in relation to your employer, have a duty 'to co-operate with him so far as is necessary to enable that duty or requirement to be performed or complied with'.[4] Therefore it is not an option for a member of staff to refuse, decline or opt out of their responsibilities within health and safety.

Your main responsibilities include:

❏ Responsibilities to staff
❏ Responsibilities to other people

---

[4] Health and Safety at Work etc. Act 1974, section 7, 'General duties of employees at work'.

Responsibilities to staff
The bulk of the responsibility rests with the employer. It is the employer who has decided to establish and run the Early Years service. It is the employer, therefore, who is charged with the duty to make sure that the environment and working practice of the people they have employed, or have agreed to be at the workplace, is healthy and safe.

Depending upon your Early Years setting, you may be both the employer and the manager (you own the business and run it), or you may be the employer (you own the business and employ someone else to run it), or be an agent of the employer (someone else owns it – local authority, charity or private company – and you are employed as a manager of it or within it).

Whichever of these scenarios matches your situation you are in some way covered by the Act and have a role that is defined as the employer at some level.

As a manager with a positive attitude to developing your staff team generally, your health and safety responsibilities will also be well served by promoting a positive culture of compliance, competence and improvement.

ACTIVITY 2.3

Having considered the responsibilities of employees, think about your employer duties. Note down a range of areas that you think such duties could touch on.

_____

_____

_____

Comment and exploration

The first principle of the law is that, as the employer, a person (you in this case) must 'ensure, so far as is reasonably practicable, the health, safety and welfare at work of all his employees'.[5]

This general duty covers a range of factors including:

- ❑ Equipment used to carry out work
- ❑ The use, storage and movement of substances needed within the working environment
- ❑ Training and information about working practices
- ❑ Record of accidents and near misses
- ❑ The physical environment, especially exits and entrances
- ❑ Adequate facilities in regards to the welfare of employees at work

Other things that you may have noted could include:

- ❑ Written policy or statement about health and safety at work (see Act, section 3)
- ❑ The right of recognised trade-union health and safety representatives to be consulted and involved in promoting and improving the practice of everyone, as well as checking on the effectiveness of current measures (see Act, sections 4, 5 and 6)
- ❑ To establish a safety committee with representatives (see Act, section 7)

---

[5] Health and Safety at Work etc. Act 1974, section 2 (1), 'General duties of employers to their employees'.

Responsibilities to other people
There is a whole range of people, other than employees, who are also covered by the Act. These include:

❏ Children who use the service
❏ Parents and carers of those children
❏ Visitors and guests
❏ Inspectors
❏ Suppliers delivering orders
❏ Employees of service companies such as electricity and water
❏ Trades people contracted to service or repair the building or equipment

You may be able to add to this list with regular or occasional visitors to your service.

Whoever comes into the work environment is covered by the Act, with section 3 setting out the employer's duty that they are not to be 'exposed to risks to their health or safety'.[6] Section 3 states that the employer must provide people other than employees with information that might affect their health or safety. You, as the manager, will need to make sure that you have actively taken steps to inform everyone about what they must do, or avoid doing, in relationship to health or safety.

Other people have a responsibility too
The Act also stipulates the duties of everyone, whether employer, employee or another person. It makes it

---

[6] Health and Safety at Work etc. Act 1974, section 3 (1), 'General duties of employers and self-employed to persons other than their employees'.

illegal to interfere with anything provided to promote health, welfare or safety within any statutory requirement.[7]

It's a strange old world!

As a manager there will be many things that you need to consider within your daily practice. There are laws you have to abide by, rules to follow, regulations to implement and choices to make.

By and large, you will undertake these within the relative privacy of your team and Early Years service. Children, parents and staff will feel the positive impact of your decisions while most of the rest of the world lets you get on with what you have to do. Occasionally inspectors of one sort or another will require you to provide evidence that all the good things that you say your service does are true, but few other people will intrude upon your busy working life.

Except, that is, unless there is a mistake made or an accident happens. In the matter of health, safety and welfare, other people will make it their business to investigate your business if things go wrong.

The following case study enables you to appreciate the benefits of hindsight...before something bad actually happens.

[7] Health and Safety at Work etc. Act 1974, section 8, 'Duty not to interfere with or misuse things provided pursuant to certain provisions'.

SCENARIO CASE STUDY

It was a normal, hectic day at Butterfly Farm Nursery. Jolene had been the manager for two years now and felt she had got to grips with the job. The team worked well together, usually – except for Daphne who sometimes seemed to do things in her own way. But as other staff told Jolene, 'We have to accept difference and diversity, don't we?'

The dishwasher was playing up once again. The only way it would work was if the plug was pushed really hard into the socket. Jolene had had it on her ever-growing 'Things To Do' list for a couple of weeks. At last the electrician had come to look at the faulty switch.

Today had been very busy. With three new children (Iain, Dasmani and Jason) starting and with full occupancy, the telephone call at 8.35 am from Mandy saying she was sick added to Jolene's pressures. All in all, though, the morning had gone quite well. The electrician had just popped out to attend to an emergency but promised to be back before the end of the day.

Now at lunchtime the extra number of children starting meant that the team needed to get more plates.

Daphne remembered that there were some in the dishwasher from yesterday. There just hadn't been time to empty it this morning. Jasmine, the recently qualified new team member, offered to fetch the plates.

Jason had stayed very close to Jasmine all morning and followed her, slipping into the kitchen area without Jasmine noticing. As she bent down to unload the dishwasher Jason tugged at her shirt. Shocked by the sudden awareness that Jason was there Jasmine turned around, losing her balance and toppling over. As she fell she reached out, knocking over the dishwasher tablet box, and knocked her head on the dishwasher.

Daphne and Jolene both responded to the noise and went into the kitchen to find Jasmine on the floor holding her head, with Jason sitting amongst the scattered dishwasher tablets, crying.

ACTIVITY 2.4

If you were the manager there would be actions that you would take in this case study. Make a note of the issues and actions you think are important.

_____

_____

_____

_____

_____

_____

Comment

Amongst the questions you might ask would be:

❏ What emergency first aid does Jasmine need for her head injury?

❏ What emergency first aid may Jason need? Is he injured physically from Jasmine's fall? Did he come into contact with the dishwasher tablets? Has he eaten any tablets?

❏ What medical treatment or opinion is required to confirm the first-aid assessments?

Depending upon the outcomes of these questions further actions would need to be considered in terms of supporting a return to normal service. In terms of the incident itself you would need to:

❏ Record the details of the incident – for the parents/carers of Jason and for the requirements of your duty to employees.

❏ Investigate the circumstances leading up to the incident to identify why it happened. Take statements from those involved (as appropriate) and record your own perceptions.

❏ Consider what appropriate actions are required to prevent a similar incident happening in future.

ACTIVITY 2.5

Apply the benefits of hindsight to the case study. What further actions would you take if you were the manager? To help you think this through you may consider what you would expect to find if you were investigating this incident.

_____

_____

_____

_____

Comment

The following points are worth considering:

❏ *Butterfly Farm Nursery* – is there a health and safety statement? If so, where is it and how effectively is it communicated? Are there risk assessments in place and are these adequate? Is there an accident and incident record in place? Is it used and are health and safety matters reviewed to help improvements to practice?

❏ *The manager* – has Jolene had any training in management of health and safety? How aware is she of her responsibilities?

❏ *The staff team* – what training or awareness is there within the team of good practice in health and safety? Is there a nominated health and safety representative (recognised trade-union member and/or team member)? Are there any new staff who have not yet received training? When was the most recent updating for established staff? What areas of health and safety did any training cover? Do staff implement their training into day-to-day practice? Has Jasmine, in the scenario, as a new member of staff, been made aware of all policies and procedures for the setting?

❏ *The kitchen environment and equipment* – was the kitchen in good order? Could anything have caused the trip or slip, e.g. floor condition, wires or equipment? What procedures are in place to maintain and check the environment and equipment to ensure everything is in good order? What records exist to demonstrate maintenance and checking procedures? Are faults reported and appropriate action taken in a timely way?

❏ *The electrician* – is s/he an employee or contractor? Did they leave the kitchen in a safe and appropriate state?

As you can see the use of hindsight is a wonderful thing! This list of questions, while not exhaustive, could potentially place responsibility for any incident on the manager (as the representative of the employer), employee or the contractor. Alternatively it could be viewed as an unforeseeable accident.

FOOD HYGIENE

The legislative framework:

The Food Safety Act 1990 and Food Safety (General Food Hygiene) Regulations 1995

The Food Standards Act 1999 (Transitional and Consequential Provisions and Savings) (England and Wales) Regulations 2000

Reference: Food Standards Agency and www.hmso.gov.uk

Do you or your staff handle food? The storage, handling, preparation or serving of food or drink will fall under this heading. So even if your service does not provide cooked lunches, the way that any food or drink is treated will need to be managed. This still applies to food or drink that is not for sale, so includes refreshments available to children, staff or visitors.

ACTIVITY 2.6

Below are some prompts for you to consider. Think about the relevance of these within your service:

Food or drink	Food-hygiene issue
Lunches provided by parent or carer	
Formula feeds	
Frozen vegetables for a prepared lunch	
Fresh meat for sandwiches or meals	
Milk for coffee or tea	
Cereal	
Donuts donated to staff by a kind parent	
Birthday cake brought in with a child	
Children making crispy chocolate cakes	
Children's milk cartons delivered at 5 am	

Comment

Some of the following headings may help you get started:

> personal hygiene
> temperature control and testing
> storage length
> kitchen hygiene
> access control
> dietary requirements and cultural taboos
> allergy information

> monitoring and recording
> training and qualification
> serving equipment

Your main responsibilities include:

❏ Ensuring that you and your staff maintain high levels of personal hygiene – e.g. hand washing before and after working with food, children's personal care
❏ Provision of equipment that promotes good hygiene – e.g. disposable gloves, appropriate bags for the disposal of waste
❏ Policies and the monitoring of procedures that ensures practice is compliant and appropriate – e.g. washing and cleaning of surfaces, temperature checks on refrigeration and freezer equipment, maintenance and repairs to ensure storage is in good order
❏ Making sure appropriate training is provided, including updating – e.g. your own organisation may deliver this, or a certified food-hygiene course can be undertaken (available from further-education colleges and private training agencies)

MANUAL HANDLING

> The legislative framework:
>
> Manual Handling Operations Regulations 1992 (as amended by the Health and Safety (Miscellaneous Amendments) Regulations 2002) (Manual Handling Regulations)
>
> Reference: www.hse.gov.uk

'Back problems are an occupational hazard in Early Years. All that bending and lifting is bound to take its toll.'

If this is a view that other managers or staff take, then you will need to get them to rethink it. Within the framework of the management of health and safety you cannot rely on practices that will, or are likely to, cause injury or harm to people employed.

The responsibilities of the manager include finding ways to get the job done without harming people.

SCENARIO CASE STUDY

'I know all about how I'm meant to do it!' Liz exploded in frustration as Kim, her team leader, reminded her once again about the technique for moving the play equipment.

'Waiting for someone else to help will just take too long. I can manage it on my own, especially if I balance it on the edge and rock it like this.'

ACTIVITY 2.7

Thinking about the scenario above, note down what you would do if you were Liz's team leader.

Comment

In real life nothing is quite like the model of 'how to manage people', not even the ones set out in this series of books! As a manager you have to consider the options and then decide what is the best way of managing for you in your context. Your working relationship with Liz may be such that you could use humour to win her around:

'Come on Liz, let me get you some help. If you do your back in just think of all those forms I'll have to fill in! You wouldn't want to make me have to do that would you?'

Or perhaps Liz could be persuaded by the facts:

'Back problems are one of the main causes of Early Years practitioners having to give up their work prematurely, Liz. I know it may take a little longer. But your health is worth it.'

Sometimes the formal approach is the only way to make staff aware that you take this very seriously.

'Liz you are not to move that equipment on your own. I am instructing you to follow the manual handling procedures.' This approach may need to be followed up by a formally recorded meeting where you reinforce this requirement.

Health and safety practice is not a choice that staff can opt in or out of. If you as the manager allow staff to use unsafe practice you will be held liable – even if they appeared to choose or prefer inappropriate methods of doing things.

Your main responsibilities include:

❏ Training and awareness raising of staff – e.g. during the induction process all staff need to be trained in the appropriate moving and handling techniques associated with their work. This will include working with children and equipment.

❏ Monitoring practice and updating – e.g. it is not enough to be able to say that 'they were trained in induction'. As the manager you need to know that the practice reflects the appropriate approaches.

❏ Provision of equipment – e.g. for some activities involving moving things there may be specialist pieces of equipment that can be used. Such things could be as simple as sliding mats.

FIRST AID

The legislative framework:

Health and Safety (First Aid) Regulations 1981

Your main responsibilities include:

❏ Ensuring that a minimum of one person is on duty at all times who is qualified in emergency first-aid procedures – this named person needs to be known to others and available to respond in an emergency

❏ Ensuring that first-aid provision covers both children and adults – some qualifications are specifically for first aid for children. To cover staff, the employer has a responsibility to provide someone fully trained in first aid at work.

❏ Ensuring that every setting has a first-aid equipment box – included must be guidance information on emergency first aid, and it must be maintained in good order by a named first aider

❏ Having a policy and procedures to gain parental consent to use emergency first aid – some parents have cultural or religious beliefs that need to be accommodated within your procedures

FIRE SAFETY

The legislative framework:

The Fire Precautions Act 1971 and Fire Precautions (Workplace) Regulations 1997

Your main responsibilities include:

❏ Ensuring that there is sufficient firefighting equipment, such as extinguishers and blankets, and that equipment is maintained and tested and of a suitable type for the nature of the risks
❏ Having clear signs to show emergency exits and ensure these pathways are kept clear
❏ Having appropriate procedures to evacuate the premises and account for those people who are evacuated
❏ Practising these procedures to ensure that staff are aware of their responsibilities and are trained to respond in an emergency

CONTROL OF SUBSTANCES HAZARDOUS TO HEALTH REGULATIONS (COSHH)

The legislative framework:

Control of Substances Hazardous to Health Regulations (COSHH) 2002

The COSHH system was brought in to raise users' awareness of the potential harm caused by use, or misuse, of substances. Health problems include harm to skin and breathing that may result from bodily contact with some chemicals found in products. Within an Early Years setting these will often be cleaning products or occasionally substances used in art or craft activities. The warning symbols use orange and black with illustrations of a cross or another appropriate symbol such as fire to indicate the type of hazard.

Spending some time looking around your own home for products with these symbols may raise your awareness of how frequently they can be found.

Your main responsibilities include:

❑ Having a record of all the products and substances within your workplace that have the COSHH symbol
❑ For each product with a COSHH symbol, having the manufacturer's information sheet in files and accessible in the event of an accident for advice on treatments (emergency services will need to refer to these)
❑ Minimising the use of substances that have a COSHH symbol – there may well be alternative products that

do not have a hazardous element but still get the job done

❏ Having clear procedures for the use and application of COSHH substances – ensure that staff are trained and implement these procedures

REPORTING OF DISEASES AND DANGER-OUS OCCURRENCES REGULATIONS (RIDDOR)

The legislative framework:

Reporting of Injuries, Diseases and Dangerous Occurrences Regulations (RIDDOR) 1995

Your main responsibilities include:

❏ Having procedures in place to report, as soon as is practicable, all incidents of death, or serious injury that results in someone being taken to hospital. This can be done using any of the following contact details:[8]
  ○ telephone 0845 300 9923 (8.30 am–5.00 pm)
  ○ fax   0845 300 9924 (anytime)
  ○ internet   www.riddor.gov.uk
  ○ email   riddor@natbrit.com
  ○ post   Incident Contact Centre, Caerphilly Business Park, Caerphilly CF83 3GG
❏ If the injury is less serious or if an illness is work related, the information needs to be communicated in writing using a specific form

---

[8] Contact details are correct at time of publishing, but readers should check for up-to-date details.

LAST THINGS FIRST – IT'S A RISKY BUSINESS

Knowing the requirements of the law is very important. This final section, however, will be vital to the health, safety and well-being of those people who share your working environment. It could also be vital for your continued development and practice as a manager.

If an accident or incident occurs, one of the first things that will be asked of you, the manager, is to provide the relevant risk-assessment documents. If you and your team have identified all known hazards, eliminated them where possible but at least recorded them, communicated to others about the hazard and put into place practices to control the risks, you will be on a strong footing. Identifying and then monitoring the progress of risk assessments is a major way that managers can show their command and level of competence in practical health and safety management.

The development of health and safety management has evolved to embrace the concept of risk assessments. In a complex and changing working environment very few procedures will remain the same year after year. In the same way that you are continually trying to improve the level of Early Years service to children and parents, you are also duty bound to check that reasonable measures are in place to minimise or eliminate risks to health and safety.

As managers we should not get this idea confused with the idea that learning involves a degree of trial and error – of learning through mistakes as well as successes. Within risk assessment of health and safety we need to identify the hazard and the controls in place.

The legislative framework:

Management of Health and Safety at Work Regulations 1999 (Management Regulations)

Reference: www.hse.gov.uk

The Health and Safety Executive provides clearly written guidance for employers and managers to follow regarding risk assessments.

Definitions

Hazard: anything that can cause harm to a person
Risk: the chance (low, medium or high) that somebody will be harmed by the hazard

A five-step process can be applied to any setting and situation. As the responsible manager you must:

1. Look for hazards – things that may cause harm to people within your workplace
2. Decide who is at risk from a hazard and how – including children, staff and visitors. Include in your thinking various actual or potential risk groups such as pregnant staff.
3. Consider the risks in the context of existing controls and procedures – are the current practices and checks appropriate? They need to be suitable and sufficient, not necessarily perfect. Take steps to strengthen existing controls if necessary.
4. Record what you have done and inform staff of the procedures to manage any identified risks
5. Periodically review the risk assessment and update it if necessary – make use of new equipment that is available or different practices that have been developed

The value of undertaking risk assessments is that hazards can be identified, eliminated or managed. The consequences of not undertaking them could be fatal or harmful to someone. This area of managerial responsibility is one of the few that can lead to legal prosecution, so getting good information and spending time leading a team that is clearly focused upon health and safety is good for everyone.

REVIEW OF – BEING HEALTHY AND STAYING SAFE

This chapter has helped you if you can

✓ Describe the main managerial responsibilities for health and safety within the workplace.
✓ Name a range of responsibility areas covering food, moving things, emergencies and prevention of accidents.
✓ Find sources to get up-to-date information and advice as a manager responsible for health and safety.
✓ Explain to your staff team why they must comply with policies and practice for the good of the children, themselves and others.

References and suggested further reading

Dare, A. and O'Donovan, M. (2000) *Good Practice in Child Safety*, Nelson Thornes.
Green, S. (2002) *BTEC National Early Years*, Nelson Thornes.
Green, S. (2003) *BTEC First Early Years*, Nelson Thornes.

Website

www.hse.gov.uk

Chapter 3

BEYOND COMPLIANCE

This chapter covers:

- The management approach to go beyond complying with the law and regulations
- The importance of the working environment for staff
- Opportunities to develop a healthy environment through a focus on customer care

You work within a highly supervised sector. You are registered, inspected, CRB checked,[1] health and safety regulated, and more. So you should be! Just think of the consequences for children if things go wrong, even occasionally.

The well-being of children, as demonstrated through an increased political focus, has been given an increasingly high priority in recent decades. Elsewhere in this book you have the chance to explore a range of requirements, such as those involved in health and safety, which are imposed upon your work. You have to get them right or else you, or your organisation or staff, will feel the legal consequences. However, the idea that a manager should feel satisfied with just *not getting it wrong* goes against the philosophy of this series of books. It should be seen as a first step to ensure that

---

[1] Criminal Records Bureau.

your service complies with what is required by the law. As a manager focused on the promotion of the best provision for the children within the care of your service, and as someone who is driven to help your staff to develop themselves, you will want to do more than just keep within the law.

A HEALTHY ENVIRONMENT

Within the UK and many other countries, the developing theme of successive governments is that Early Years provision is key in promoting the right start in life for the new generation. This view continues unchallenged. Along with a concern about the impact of changing habits of individuals and within society generally on the physical development and the general health of the population at large goes an interest about diet and the promotion of a 'healthy lifestyle'.

Governments are concerned with the health of their nation, the costs of medical and social care, and the impact on economic prosperity in the future. You and your staff team are more likely to be focused upon the children you know and work with everyday and, to some extent, their families and communities.

As a manager, you, along with politicians and other policy-makers, will therefore be interested in the answer to this question:

How well does your service promote a healthy lifestyle?

To explore answers to this question you can focus on:

❑ Children
❑ Staff and other adults

In many cases the same or similar approaches will be taken to both groups.

In the rest of this chapter we will concentrate on your managerial responsibilities and opportunities with staff and other adults.

WORKING SPACE

The place of work, for many people, will be somewhere that you spend the majority of your waking days. During a normal working week most staff on full-time contracts will be 'at work' for somewhere between 37 and 45 hours. This is a large amount of time to spend in a single place.

Your surroundings will have an impact on you and

how well you work. Individual members of your staff team may well have a specialist area within the work environment that means they have an even smaller space that they occupy for the majority of their working time.

ACTIVITY 3.1

Think about the sorts of things that are important to people and the space in which they operate. Note down some of the things about a working environment that you consider are important to promote efficiency and effectiveness.

_____

_____

_____

Comment

The working environment has a major impact on how people feel about their work and how motivated they are.[2] You may have identified ideas like:

❏ The amount of space available to work in
❏ The light (natural or electric) and heat controls
❏ The number of other occupants and noise levels
❏ Opportunities to make it a personal or 'owned' space
❏ The feeling of control over the environment

If people feel that they have some form of long-term relationship with the space they work in they

---

[2] See another of our books in this series, _Managing People and Teams._

will usually feel more positive. This ownership will be enhanced if an individual has some degree of control over personal issues such as temperature, access, decoration or displays.

In some cases individual staff may not be able to decide on all these environmental factors. It is worth considering to what extent opportunities to share decision-making can be engineered.

GENERAL ENVIRONMENT

The community in which your service operates will have an impact upon those people who live in it and use it. To test out the impact on you of the general environment in which you work think about the journey in the morning. How do you feel about going to work? Does the journey pass calmly and allow you to ease into the day, or is your experience more one of growing tension? How do you feel as you leave the external environment and enter into your organisation's space? Do other staff, parents and children experience similar feelings? What effect does this have on the mood of people?

It may be that the external environment generates positive feelings and that your challenge is to encourage them to continue as people come through the door into your Early Years service. Alternatively, it could be that the task is more to do with creating an oasis where people can find respite from the outside world.

It is worth thinking about this issue as it can prove to be a vital marketing advantage. Many parents will choose Early Years provision due to a combination of factors, one of which is 'it felt like the right place'.

The first impression of the reception area will have a large impact on setting the tone for your whole service.

ACTIVITY 3.2

Test your reception area. The next time you go to work try focusing upon the general environment outside and its effect on how you feel. Next consciously consider the impact on you of the entrance and reception area as you go into work. If you were a child, parent or member of staff what message about the service would you pick up?

Comment

You may benefit from asking others about their opinions of the external environment and the first impression of the entrance area. This can be useful feedback from visiting adults such as candidates after the recruitment process or visiting professionals and parents.

Once you form a view about the impact of the parts of the general environment and entrance area that you can influence, you will need to decide what to improve or make sure remains in place.

CUSTOMER CARE – THE CULTURE OF YOUR SERVICE

The physical environment is very important to the way that people feel. As important, or perhaps even more important, is the way in which people are treated as this will have an impact on the emotional well-being of children, parents and staff alike. As the manager you will need to take measures to establish a positive team culture where the focus is upon excellent service.

If someone asked you to describe the way that customers within your service were treated and dealt with, what would you answer?

The way in which parents and children who are regular users of your service are welcomed every day, shown respect and interest, given time and information, and cared for and included will have an important impact on how your service is perceived by staff, parents and children.

The way that potential customers are treated will also be important to the service. Treating potential customers well by showing them the type of healthy and safe environment in which you will provide excellent care and education for their child is key to continuing business.

Do you have a similar or varied approach to regular

and potential customers? Some commercial organisations differentiate between the two. In an effort to attract more new custom they appear to provide extra care or benefits. If you think about banks, credit-card companies or supermarkets, you may be able to identify promotional activities they use to attract new customers – discounts, offers and accepting a rival's vouchers have all been used to tempt people to change brands. Once attracted, the hope is that the service, environment and products (or, in some cases, apathy of the customer) will result in loyalty of custom.

Early Years provision is not quite the same. Finding new customers is important to replace the children who will grow up and move on. The complexity and emotional investment that parents place in care and education for their children usually means that while first impressions are important the ongoing experience for the child and parent is vital. Putting on a show for open days or viewings must achieve the right balance between sharing the good things about your service

and being sure that you and your team will consistently deliver that level of service.

ACTIVITY 3.3

Talk with members of your team about their view of the customer-care culture of the team. How good, how consistent, how customer focused is their work? What examples can people recall of where customer care could have been better, and how?

Next select some customers to listen to. The focus of this exercise is to listen to their perceptions about their experiences of your service. It is not a time to argue or point out what they did that may have been a problem for you. Such listening activities can be very valuable as a market-research activity. For example, you may think that the cheerful and friendly manner with which your team engage parents at the start of the day, providing infor- mation about the planned activities and lunch options for that day, is great customer care. However, some parents may tell you that they don't have time for that in the morning rush.

Comment

As a result of listening to your staff and to your customers you can form a view about what should be maintained and what needs to be developed.

This approach may bring to your attention a range of views, some of which you may disagree with, while others may confirm your own thinking.

The important thing for a manager is to evaluate the information you collect and decide what is the next step towards your overall aim of creating and maintaining a healthy and positive working environment.

REVIEW OF – BEYOND COMPLIANCE

This chapter has helped you if you can

✓ Start to consider opportunities within your service to measure and improve the environment for children, parents and staff.

References and suggested further reading

Blanchard, K. and O'Connor, M. (1997) *Managing by Values*, Berrett-Koehler.

Peters, T. and Austin, N. (1989) *A Passion for Excellence*, Fontana.

INDEX